D1130020

20 Progressive Fingerstyle Studies for Uke by Rob MacKillop

CD contents

1 2 3 4 5 6 7 8 9 0

Visit us on the Web at www.melbay.com — E-mail us at email@melbay.com

Contents

Introduction

The ukulele has come a long way in recent years, with performances in movies, in the charts, and all over YouTube. The attraction of the instrument is that it is easy to pick up and within a short period of time you are able to strum a few simple chords and hundreds of songs. Many of my students begin this way, but I have found that after a few months some of them start looking for something a little more challenging to play. It was for them I started writing fingerstyle arrangements – see my other Mel Bay ukulele books – and to play those pieces well it became clear that a set of studies would be of use, hence the present set of twenty progressive studies on all aspects of fingerstyle playing on the ukulele.

You will find here studies in different styles – blues, jazz, classical, and even minimalism and serialism. There are studies in arpeggios, scales, modes, ii-V-I chord sequences, strumming, syncopation, campanella fingerings, improvisation, hammer-ons and pull-offs. Some of the studies concentrate on the left hand, some on the right hand, some on both. I believe this is the most comprehensive set of studies currently available for the ukulele, mastery of which will equip you to explore any style of music you wish. It is also a showcase for how well the ukulele can adapt to different styles of music.

The ukulele is an extraordinary instrument, with a remarkable history. Apart from its well-practiced use as a strummed accompaniment instrument, it is capable of real beauty, and the most delicate expression. It has as much depth as Renaissance and Baroque guitars and lutes, and is worthy of serious study by all those who have a heart for music.

The whole book is dedicated to the mighty uke!

Good luck!

Rob MacKillop
Edinburgh

Performance Notes

Study 1 – Scale Time

Learning scales need not be a chore. Here we have a basic C Major scale given a twist with some syncopated timing. 'Syncopated' means having accents where they do not normally fall. In a bar of 4/4 timing there is usually an accent in beats One and Three – ONE and two and THREE and four. 'Scale Time' plays with our expectations. The first bar starts with an accent on ONE, but thereafter things get a little surprising:
ONE and two AND three AND four AND

Each of the first three bars has different accents. Despite this complexity, the whole thing should flow effortlessly. Try to work it out before listening to the soundfile.

Study 2 – Waiting For Anthony

I wrote this while waiting for my student, Anthony, to arrive for his lesson. It's a simple study for the right hand, so make sure you follow the right-hand indications: T = Thumb, i = index, m = middle.

Bar 9 introduces a little dissonance – as my patience was wearing thin! 'Dissonance' means notes which don't sound quite like they belong there. Its opposite is consonance. Try to be aware at all times whether you are playing consonant or dissonant notes.

Study 3 – Somewhere Under The Rainbow

A little tribute to IZ, whose version of Somewhere Over The Rainbow did much to popularise the uke in recent years.

The open middle pair of strings are sounded throughout the whole piece, and are plucked with the index and middle fingers. The ring finger plucks all the notes on the first string, with the thumb playing all the notes on the fourth string.

Try to keep the inner strings quieter than the outer strings.

Bar 10 introduces a quintuplet – five quick notes on one beat. This will take quite a bit of practice to get right.

Study 4 – Hawaiian Landscape With Rain

The most important bar in this study is the first. Experience has shown that most students rush through it to get to where the action is. But setting the scene is very important, otherwise the first note on the first string in Bar 2 will miss its mark.

This study is written in a style known as minimalism.

Study 5 – 251

The numbers 2, 5 and 1 refer to the most common harmonic movement in Western music for the last 400 years. In the key of C, this would be Dm, G7 and C. Entire books have been compiled of various ways of playing these chords, very often with altered notes here and there to spice things up. Jazz players dedicate many hours of their lives to negotiating the progression. By way of an introduction to the myriad of possibilities, I offer two typical lines. Jazz can sound great on the ukulele.

Study 6 – 332

This study introduces an unusual time signature: 3 + 3 + 2 over 8. This looks complicated, but it could have been more familiarly written as 4/4. Then why the complicated version? It shows the groupings of quarter notes (quavers) used throughout the whole study. Try to place a subtle accent on the 'one' of each group.

The repeat of the whole study calls for false harmonics. This is how to play the first note with a false harmonic. Hold the note down with the left hand first finger, as usual. The right hand is a little unusual. Place the index finger on the string 12 frets above the left hand note (in this case, fret 13). Don't press the string down with the right hand, just let the finger rest gently on the string. Now pluck the string with the right hand ring finger, which will produce a harmonic. Remove the right hand index finger once the note has sounded.

Study 7 – I Afreeka

This is a very rhythmical and percussive study, inspired by a political movement in Africa promoting non violence. The movement is not aligned to any political party; instead the individual makes an absolute commitment not to use violence as a means to social change.

Some of my students have found the technique of tapping the strings with the index finger a difficult one. Listen closely to the sound file.

The time signature is 10/8, and could have been written as 3 + 3 + 2 + 2.

Importantly, repeat each bar as many times as you like, and play the bars in any order you like.

Study 8 – Airpeggios

The challenge here is to extract a melody from an accompaniment. The right hand should be sensitive enough and controlled enough to play melodies and accompaniments at different volumes. You must also make a decision about which notes are melody notes, and which are accompaniment notes. Try to work it out before listening to the soundfile.

Study 9 – C

This study is in two sections, each with its own right-hand pattern. Practise each pattern separately on open strings.

Each bar has one or more fixed chord positions for each pattern. Memorise these chord shapes as quickly as possible, practising them as block chords just rolled with the right hand thumb. Eventually put the left-hand shapes and the right-hand patterns together.

The thumb plays the melody throughout, so try to pluck it a little louder than the other notes.

Study 10 – Campanology

Baroque guitar players such as the Spaniard, Gaspar Sanz, were fond of playing notes of a scale on different strings. The Baroque guitar tuning used by Sanz had the third string as the lowest note, the fourth and fifth string being higher pitched. This is called re-entrant tuning, and is similar to how we normally tune the ukulele. This study explores C Major scale, starting each bar on a different note, and maps the notes across the strings rather that climbing up one or two strings. Allow the notes to overlap where possible – this clashing of sounds can be very *appealing* – the campanella effect.

The study also includes a number of slurs: hammer-ons and pull-offs. Always make the first note of a slur louder than the subsequent note.

Starting the same scale on a different note introduces the concept of modes. A mode is an area of a scale. The first bar starts on C – the Ionian mode. The second starts on D – the Dorian mode. The third starts on E – the Phrygian mode. The fourth starts on F – the Lydian mode. The fifth starts on G – the Mixolydian mode.

If you like this style, see my Mel Bay edition, *20 Spanish Baroque Pieces by Gaspar Sanz arranged for Ukulele*.

Study 11 – Tri-Cycle

This study shows one way of playing the Cycle of 5ths on the ukulele. If you take any chord, by turning it int a 7th chord – e.g. C becomes C7 – you can 'cycle' around all possible keys. A 7th chord usually falls to a chord 5 notes away (or four if you count up the way) – C Bb A G F: C7 to F. That F now becomes F7, and falls to Bb. That Bb becomes Bb7 and falls to Eb, and so on, until you eventually find yourself back at C. Experiment with this study. Play block chords. Play arpeggios. Use different time signatures. Strum. Just try t get the sound of the cycle of triads (the Tri-Cycle) in your head. You will start to hear it in songs on the radio and elsewhere. Composers have been using it for many years.

Study 12 – How About A Little Blues?

The studies have been getting a little 'heavy' of late, so here is a little finger-picking blues to lighten the moo – yes, the blues can be enlightening.

The written timing is difficult and misleading – best listen to the soundfile many times. The downbeat (the first beat) of many of the bars is anticipated – as at the very beginning of the piece. And the quavers are played in a style known as 'jazz triplets' – difficult to notate, but hopefully easy to hear and then play. I've tried to put in lots of clichés, which you could steal and use in your own blues. That's what all good blue players do and have done for decades.

Study 13 – The Tonemeister

This unusual study is written in the style known as 12-Tone or serialism. It was a method of organising all twelve semitones in a way that could be used for compositional purposes. A 'tone row' is chosen, using all twelve semitones (sometimes fewer), then each note is assigned a number, 1 to 12. Through various manipula tions of this tone row, other rows are created.

I wanted to involve you in the creation of this piece. Your task is to play the notes in any rhythm of your choosing. This could be a regular rhythm, like 4/4, or one of the 'compound' rhythms such as 3+3+2, or 'arhythmically' – no specific rhythm at all, as I did on my soundfile performance. Each time you play this piece it should sound different. The difficulty is in making the largely dissonant melodies sound 'musical'.

Study 14 – Spider Crawl

Here is a left-hand study which is used by many professionals on many string instruments. When executed properly, it has been likened visually to a spider crawling up the neck of your instrument!

The first four quarter (quaver) notes show the pattern that will be repeated at different frets. Study these four diads (two-note chords) carefully, playing them over and over before proceeding to the rest of the study.

Each left-hand finger moves in a different direction at the same time. It is therefore a really useful exercise for developing finger independence.

Study 15 – Susan's Foot-tapping Waltz

This is a study in alternating 2/4 and 6/8 rhythms. Count:

One and Two and

One and a Two and a   …with each line repeated, as each bar is repeated.

I saw my wife's foot tapping out the rhythm while doing knitting!

Study 16 – Seven Campanella Major Scales

A study in campanella scale playing, but in a layout that could be useful when improvising. For instance: play G7 chord, then play the C Major scale line, ending with a C chord. You don't have to play the whole line, maybe just half of it, or as much of it as you feel you want to.

Memorize these runs. You will find many uses for them when you come to improvising.

Study 17 – The No. 1 Ladies Detective Agency Dance

The No. 1 Ladies' Detective Agency is a novel by Alexander McCall Smith. This study along with studies 6 and 7 forms a mini 'African Suite', and could be performed as such. It is in 'Rondo' form: that is, the first two bars could be played after bar 3, bar 4, bar 5 and bar 6, as well as at the end. The soundfile will make the form clear.

Study 18 – The Blue Uke

My first ukulele was a Gretsch, with a round, blue body. My grandfather sent me it from his home in San Diego, along with the 'Fun With Ukulele' book by Mel Bay. It was my first instrument, and set me on the road to a life in music. Here is a little blues study in memory of it.

There are lots of slurs, which need to be executed cleanly. The study does not follow the 12-bar blues format, but any of the licks could be incorporated in the standard form in the key of C.

Study 19 – In Training

Another 'minimalist' piece (see Study 4), this time very fast and busy from the outset. It is heavily influenced by the music of Steve Reich. It gets pretty fast towards the end, so don't set out too quickly, as there should be no slowing down.

Study 20 – Bar Dance

This is a study in both the left hand barré, and a common right-hand strumming pattern. Practise each separately as well as together.

Barrés or 'bar chords' can be tricky – though less so on the uke than the guitar. Make sure your left-hand thumb is supporting your index finger underneath the neck, and that your middle finger is not leaning into (or worse, on top of!) your index finger barré.

The right-hand strumming pattern is thumb down, index up, index down. Strum on the neck of the instrument, near to the 12th fret, rather than over the soundhole.

There are three bonus CD tracks: Study 17 at double speed; Study 17 at half speed; Study 2 'in echo'. I just like the sound of them!

1. Scale Time

Rob MacKillop ©2009

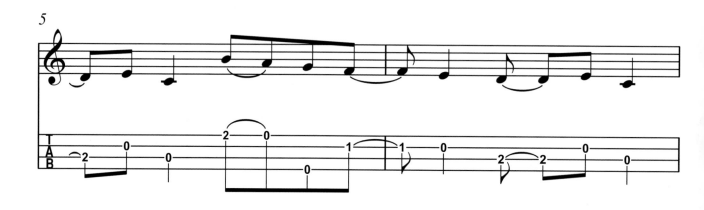

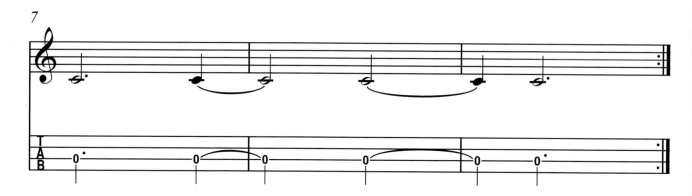

2. Waiting For Anthony

Rob MacKillop ©2009

Play each bar four times, except final bar

3. Somewhere Under The Rainbow

Rob MacKillop© 2009

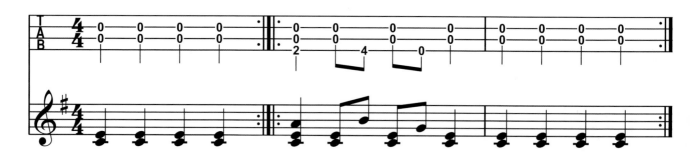

4

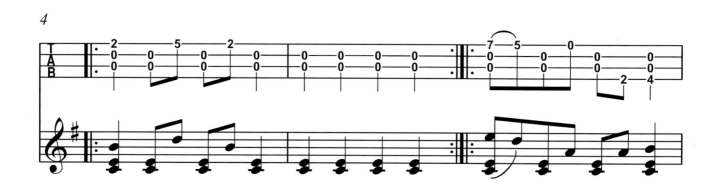

7

Repeat whole piece from Bar 2

Repeat whole piece from Bar 2

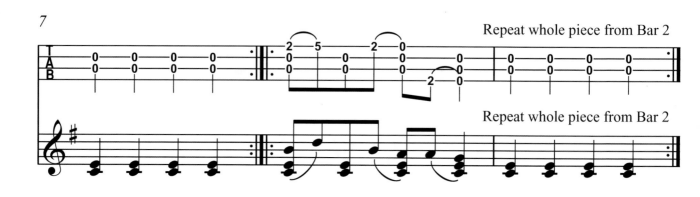

10

Many times and fade

Many times and fade

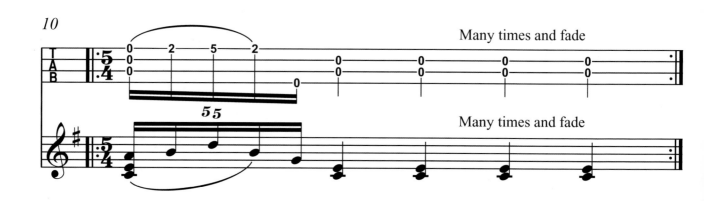

4. Hawaiian Landscape With Rain
(Homage to Leo Brouwer)

Rob MacKillop©

Track 5

5. 251

Rob MacKillop ©2009

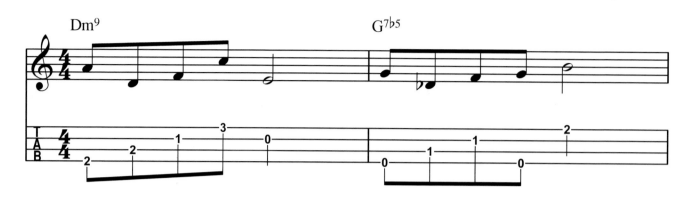

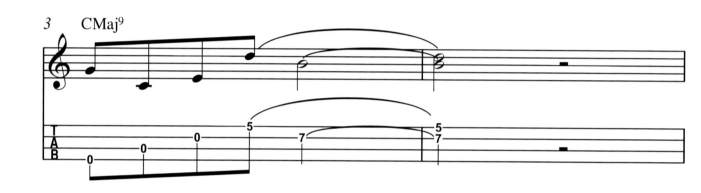

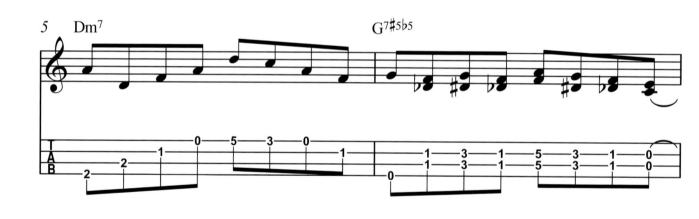

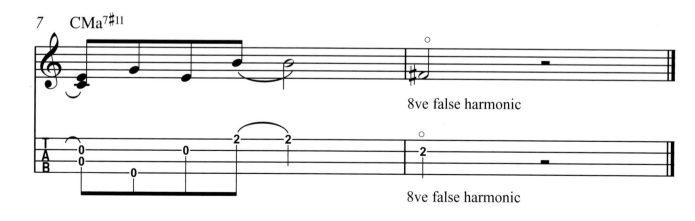

6. 332

Rob MacKillop ©2009

Play whole piece twice, but 2nd time play false harmonics except on fourth string

(x4)

(x2)

7. Afreeka

Rob MacKillop ©2009

Very rhythmical - tap the strings with the right hand near the soundhole and sometimes near the bridge. When tapping the B section, allow the RH finger to tap the soundboard as well as the strings. The three sections are interchangeable *ad lib.*

8. Airpeggios

Rob MacKillop ©2009

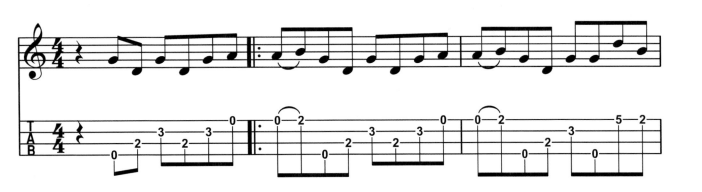

4

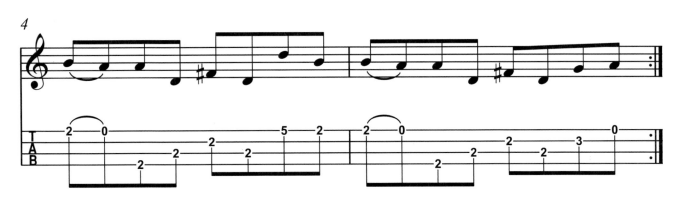

6

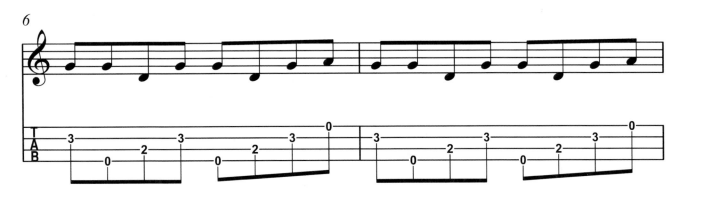

8

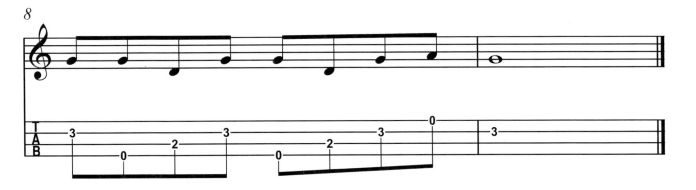

9. C

Rob MacKillop ©2009

Track 10

10. Campanology

Rob MacKillop ©2009

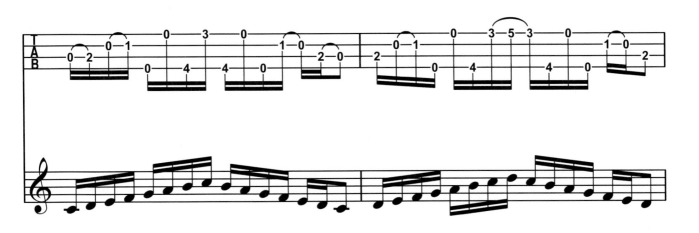

3

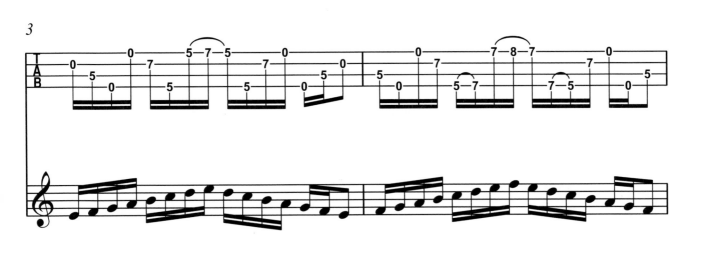

5

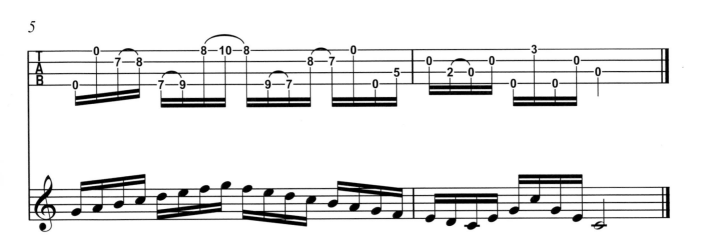

11. Tri-Cycle

Rob MacKillop ©2009

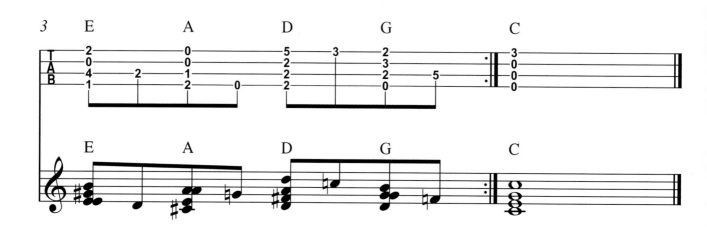

This is the Cycle of Fourths or Fifths - a way of moving smoothly through all twelve keys by turning each Tonic into a Dominant Seventh of the next chord. There are other fingerings and chord voices which could be used.

First, play as written, and then try various right hand arpeggio patterns, maybe strumming, changing the timing and rhythms. Explore.

This page has been left blank to avoid awkward page turns.

12. How About A Little Blues?

Rob MacKillop ©2009

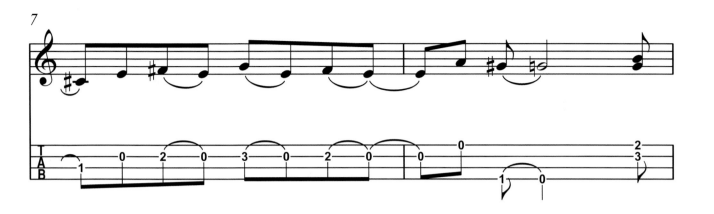

Improvise rhythms to this 12-Tone Row series. The exercise is in learning to phrase single-note chromatic lines. You could be arhythmic, or in a repetitive rhythm like jig-time, or both, or 7/8, etc....
This style of composition is known as 12-Tone or serialism.
Try analysing it! Then write your own...

13. The Tonemeister

Rob MacKillop ©2009

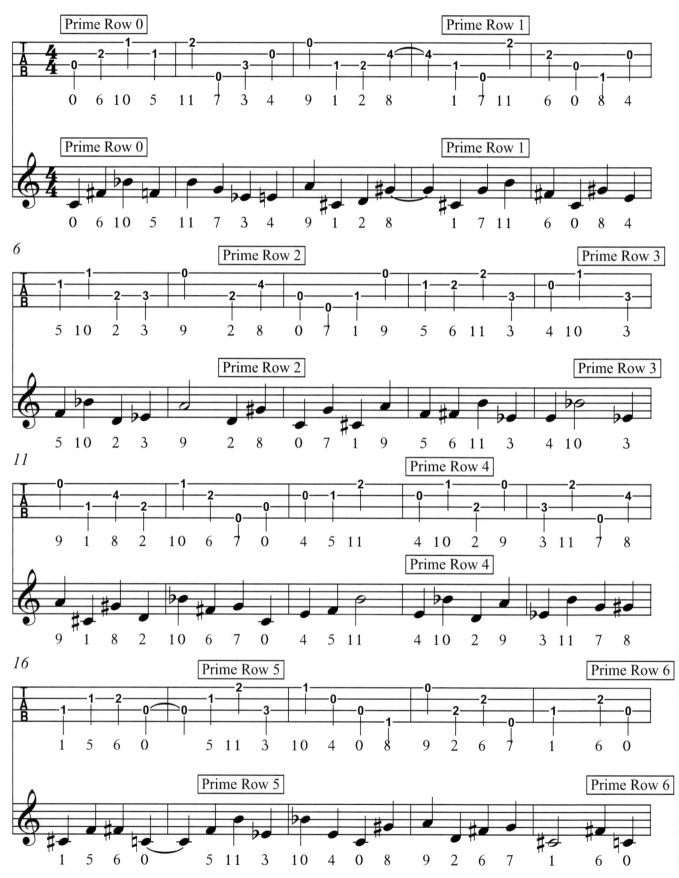

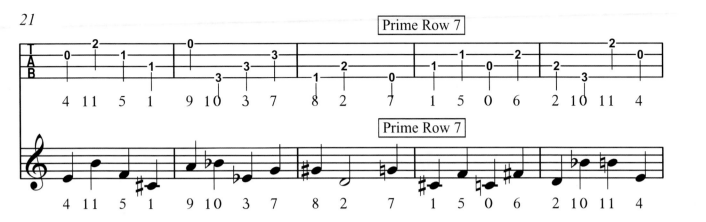

Prime Row 7

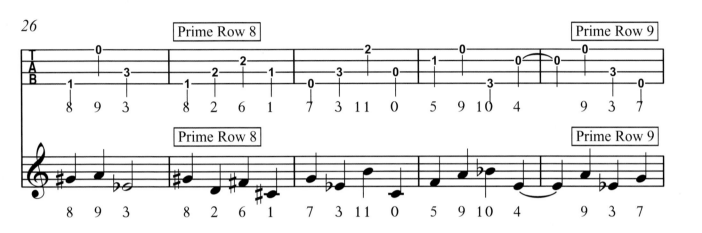

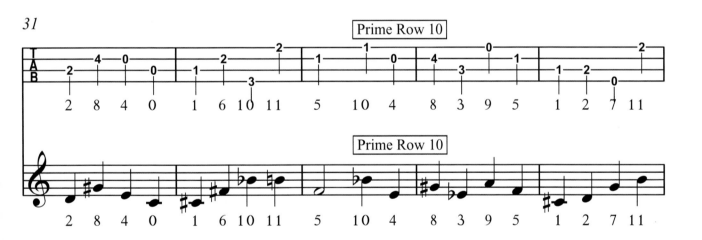

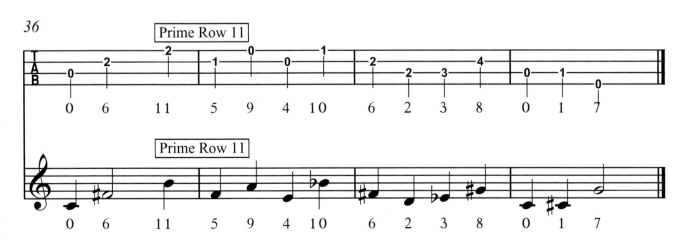

14. Spider Crawl

Rob MacKillop ©2009

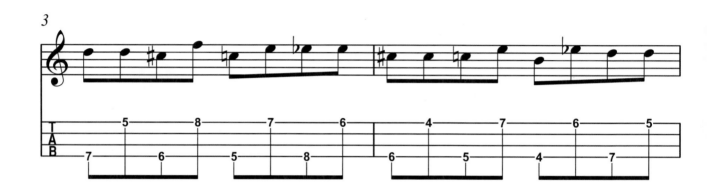

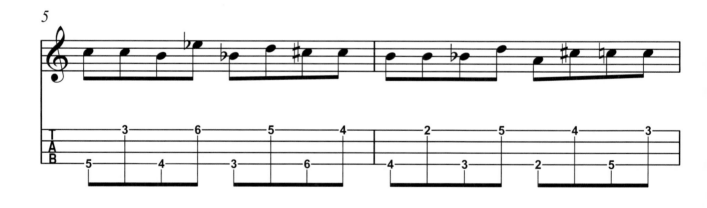

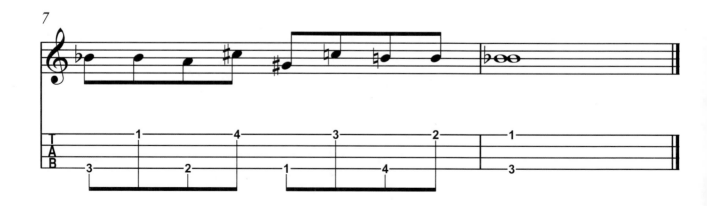

This page has been left blank to avoid awkward page turns.

15. Susan's Foot-Tapping Waltz

Rob MacKillop ©2009

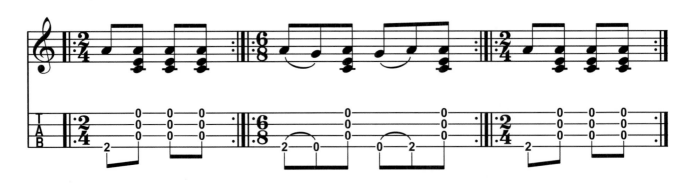

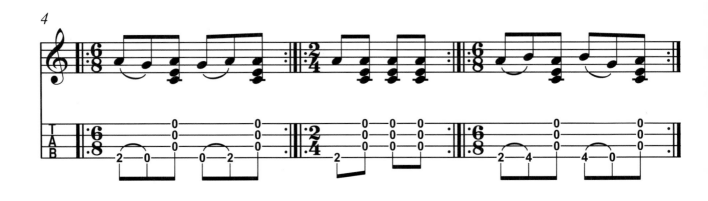

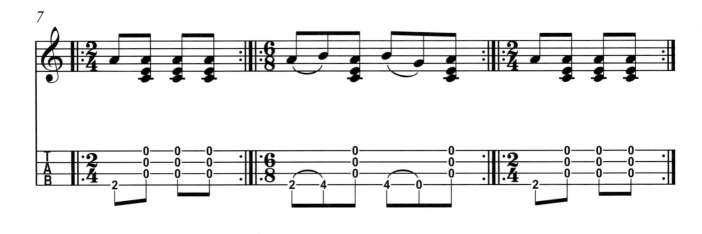

Repeat the last two bars *ad infinitum*

16. Seven Campanella Major Scales

Rob MacKillop ©2009

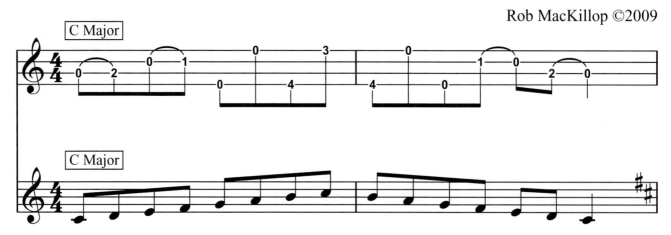

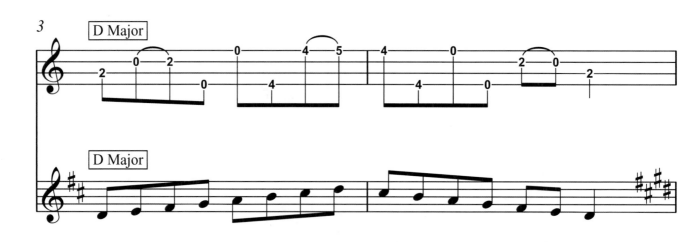

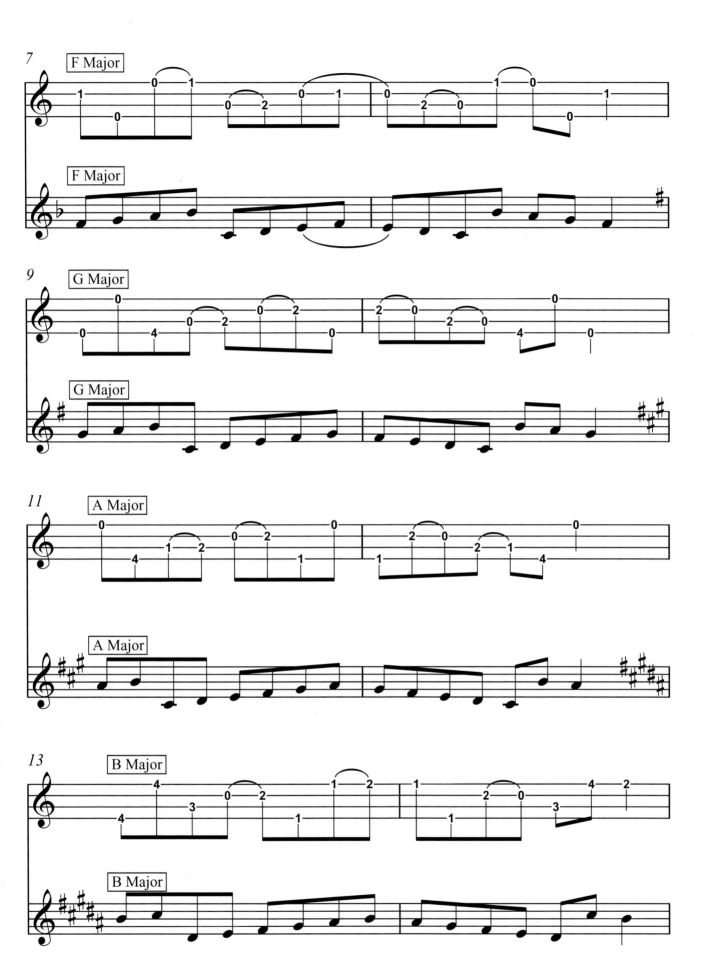

17. The No. 1 Ladies Detective Agency Dance

Rob MacKillop ©2009

Track 17

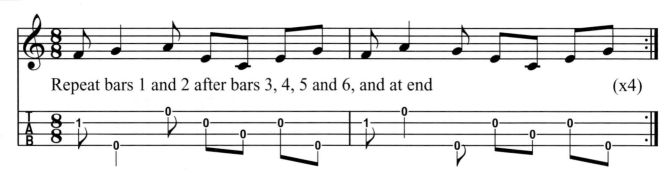

Repeat bars 1 and 2 after bars 3, 4, 5 and 6, and at end   (x4)

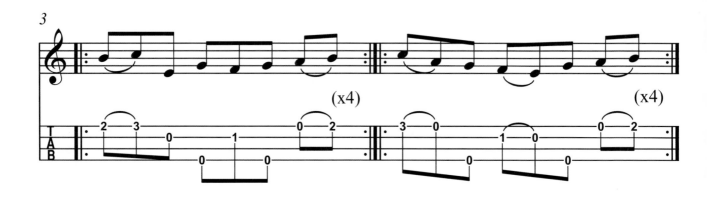

(x4)   (x4)

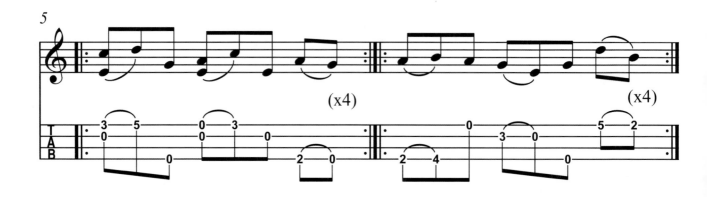

(x4)   (x4)

Repeat this line a few times starting slow and getting faster and faster...
then play bars 1 and 2 four times, fading to nothing

(x2)   (x2)   (x2)   (x2)

18. The Blue Uke

Rob MacKillop©

FORM: A B A C D

Quite fast

19. In Training

Rob MacKillop ©2009

Repeat each bar a few times *ad lib.*

20. Bar Dance

Rob MacKillop ©2009

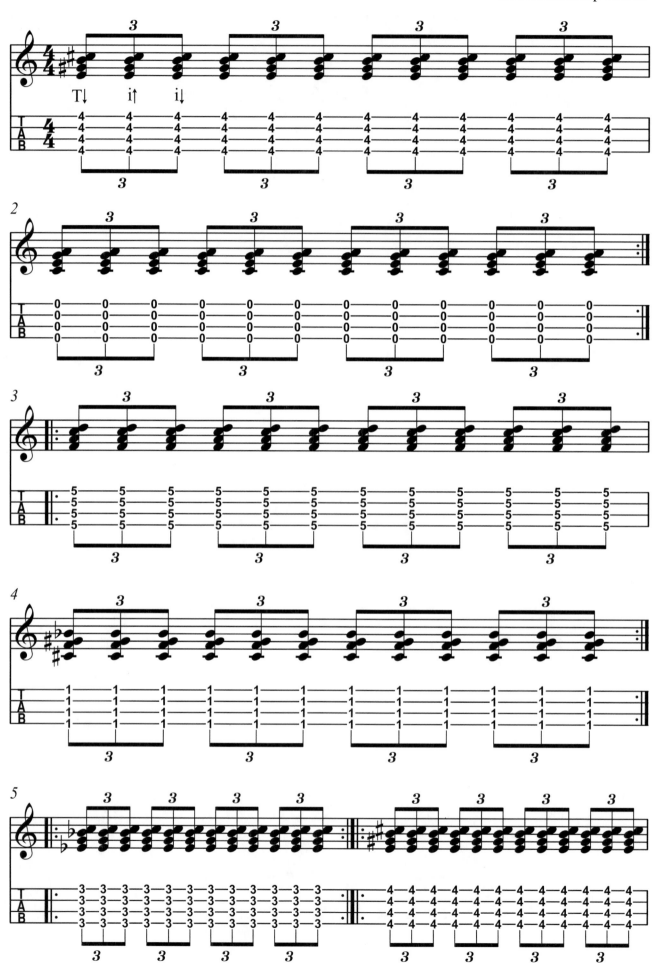

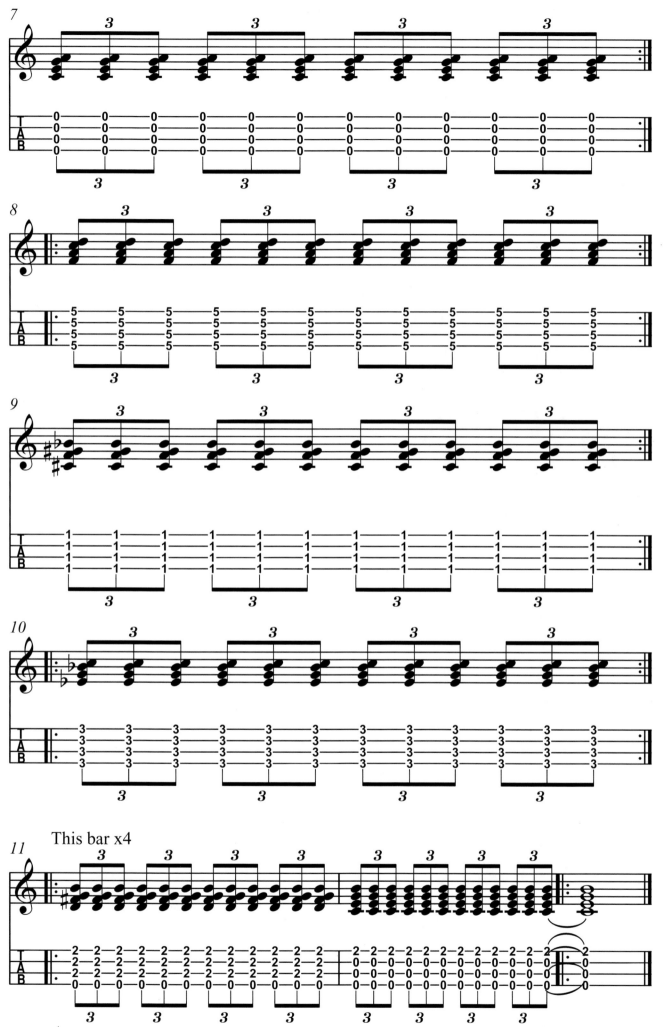

Rob MacKillop

"One of Scotland's finest musicians" *Celtic World*
"A top-drawer player" *Early Music Today*
"A true champion of Scottish music" *The Herald*
"A player of real quality, with warmth of personality and communication skills to match...one of Scotland's top professionals" *Classical Guitar*
"MacKillop displays dazzling virtuosity...the playing is exceptionally musical" *Sounding Strings*
"a leading traditional talent who is single-handedly responsible for unearthing some of the nation's finest music" *The Scotsman*

Photo by Susan Rennie

Rob MacKillop has recorded eight CDs of historical music, three of which reached the Number One position in the Scottish Classical Music Chart. In 2001 he was awarded a Churchill Fellowship for his research into medieval Scottish music, which led him to studying with Sufi musicians in Istanbul and Morocco. He broadcast an entire solo concert on BBC Radio 3 from John Smith's Square, London.

He has presented academic papers at conferences in Portugal and Germany, and has been published many times. Rob has been active in both historical and contemporary music.

Three of Scotland's leading contemporary composers have written works for him, and he also composes new works himself. In 2004 he was Composer in Residence for Morgan Academy in Dundee, and in 2001 was Musician in Residence for Madras College in St Andrews. He created and Directed the Dundee Summer Music Festival.

He worked as a Reader of schools literature for Oxford University Press, and as a reviewer for *Music Teacher*. He has also been Lecturer in Scottish Musical History at Aberdeen University, Dundee University, and at the Royal Scottish Academy of Music and Drama, and for five years worked as Musician In Residence to Queen Margaret University in Edinburgh. He has been a regular article writer for BMG magazine.

Rob plays banjo, guitar and ukulele with gut strings, plucking the strings with the flesh of his fingers, not the nails. This produces a warm and intimate sound, reminiscent of the old lute players.

www.robmackillop.net

Checkout www.MelBay.com for more editions by Rob MacKillop